Still Within My Heart

A Book for the Grieving

Deborah P. Hammond-Watts, Ph.D.

Copyright © 2020

Still Within My Heart
by
Deborah P. Hammond-Watts, Ph.D.

ISBN-13: 978-1949084092

FIRST EDITION
2020

DEDICATION

In loving memory…to my late husband,
parents, relatives and friends…

I miss you…I love you…and
you are **<u>still</u>** within my heart!

*"Tis better to have loved and lost than
never to have loved at all".*

Alfred Lord Tennyson

To Everything There is a Season...

To everything there is a season, and a time to every purpose under the heaven:

A time to be born, and a time to die; a time to plant, and a time to pluck up that which is planted;

A time to kill, and a time to heal; a time to break down, and a time to build up;

A time to weep, and a time to laugh; a time to mourn, and a time to dance;

A time to cast away stones, and a time to gather stones together; a time to embrace, and a time to refrain from embracing;

A time to get, and a time to lose; a time to keep, and a time to cast away;

A time to rend, and a time to sew; a time to keep silence, and a time to speak;

A time to love, a time to hate; a time of war, and a time of peace.

Ecclesiastes 3:1-8 ASV

INTRODUCTION

If you are reading this book, I am sorry for your loss and the pain you are now feeling. The pain will lessen with time, even though you may be wondering at this very moment, how that could possibly be true. The pain is because of a lost love – the relationship experienced with that person will determine the degree of pain experienced and the length of time required for healing. Therefore, the personal journey of healing will vary for each individual. Try not to compare your healing journey with another who may have experienced loss of a loved one around the same period of time. Each is forever changed in a manner one never could have imagined! May your faith in God bring much needed comfort as you heal. I am hopeful the information within brings you understanding and peace… which will eventually allow you to smile; as your loved one remains forever within your heart.

CONTENTS

GRIEF AND MOURNING

Grief is a multifaceted response to loss, particularly to the loss of someone or something that has died, to which a bond or affection was formed (Wikipedia, 2020). For those who have experienced grief, it is a hurt like no other, it is an overwhelming pain that is not wished upon one's worst enemy. The sadness and pain of grief can never be forgotten as it brings along an overwhelming feeling of dread. Grief is a feeling that is wrapped up and put away inside; it remains forever from the very first visit. Trying to stifle it will only make its effort to present itself more persistent. Your persistence to stifle grief and its persistence to present itself is a battle the human form is incapable of winning. You'll learn that grief will make itself known at the cost of your emotional and physical health. Once you realize and accept that the battle is not yours, you will succumb and allow yourself to grieve; as you will have learned; there is no other choice.

Mourning refers to a time of sadness because of a loss. Google (2020) defines mourning as an expression of deep sorrow for someone who has died; typically involving following certain conventions such as wearing black clothing. Grieving deals with the emotion death of a loved one brings forward and mourning deals with the action of displaying that grief. When one stops wearing black clothing it does not necessarily mean the person is no longer grieving. Brighter colored clothing may have replaced black causing another to think the person is better and moving forward from grief. However, the affect of the individual grieving may indicate an emotional state that should not be ignored. The world mourns the death of hundreds of thousands of people in numerous countries due to a pandemic. A nation mourns the death of its president and the national flag is flown at half mast. The entrance door to the Police Precinct is draped in black and purple bunting to indicate mourning following the death of a fellow officer killed in the line of duty. The door to the Fire Station is draped in black and purple bunting to indicate mourning after the death of a fellow fire fighter. A set of Congo drums is draped in black bunting to indicate mourning following the death of the musician that played them. What other actions can you list that may indicate mourning the deceased? How long does one demonstrate they are in mourning by wearing black clothing? When the bunting is removed from an object or the door of the building, has mourning of the co-worker ceased? What is considered an adequate time to mourn a loss?

Grief is a natural response to loss. It is the emotional suffering one feels when something or someone a person loves is taken away. Individuals grieve in connection with a variety of losses throughout their lives including but not limited to unemployment, foreclosure, relocation, loss of a pet, ill health, the end of a romantic relationship and or the loss of "normalcy" after a stay at home order by the government in the midst of a pandemic. Many of us have grieved the loss of the family pet and wondered how we could ever replace it by bringing another pet into our home. We knew we could not "replace" that particular animal, but we could bring another pet into our home to love. How many of us have had our hearts broken by a boyfriend or girlfriend that no longer wanted to be with us? We wondered how we could possibly go on; that is, until the next cute girl or boy wandered down the halls of our high school or on the grounds of our college campus? How many have gone through divorce? No one ever marries thinking their union will end and bring a halt to the family life being built. Yet, we recover and learn that life goes on; that we are better off because one door closing allowed one to open and usher in another opportunity to love, to create happy times and wonderful memories. We also grieve at the thought of what is to come. We anticipate the death of a loved one as hospice care becomes part of the family discussion as death, according to the doctors, is imminent. Are there other instances where you have felt as if a particular loss was devasting at the time? How did you heal and go on with your life? Crying is a normal natural response to grief. Talking and writing about losses are also healthy responses that work to assist the body in finding mechanisms to deal with reality. The feelings of loss can build into strong emotions for the body to handle as it must find a manner for release. Some individuals may be very demonstrative in their display of such emotions while others may be just the opposite and appear almost "zombie" like.

Grieving is a personal process that has no imposed time limit or correct way to express the emotion. Depending on the relationship with the deceased, one could grieve for a number of years. The survivor must learn to live in the world, often the same environment, without their lost love. It is a daunting task for the survivor to figure out how to manage day to day when the person lost was an integral part of their everything. It is unimaginable to visualize the importance of someone to your everyday existence, that is, until they are no longer around to fill the void their absence creates. The silence created by the void is very loud; so much so that it cannot and will not be ignored.

After a period of grieving, one may be able to function day to day without traces of grief appearing outward to others. The survivor may even feel as if they are managing well. This is usually the point when an unexpected reminder shows up. A reminder that will not let that person forget who they have now become; one who loved and lost. Reminders seem to appear out of nowhere... a credit application requests marital status; information for the U.S. Census requests the number of people living in the household; the clerk at the flower shop wants to know the color flower you'll need for Mother's Day; a home repairman asks to speak with your husband; the painter asks which color your wife would prefer, a vacation reminder in preparation for the two of you to celebrate an anniversary pops up on your cell phone... Evenings and nights seem to go on forever as there is no one to share a laugh, the evening meal or to discuss events of the day. Grief has turned your familiar world into the unfamiliar. Grief may leave your being for moments only to return to inner thoughts with reminders of who you are now and what you carry within. Sometimes the reminders seem to come with a vengeance. Unfortunately, grief is not likely to ever go away completely. Holiday and anniversary grief can go on seemingly forever, always placing the loved one at the forefront of memory of those special dates and times. The loved one is within forever in one form or another and your mind will not let you forget that. Grief is now a part of your being simply because you loved another deeply.

Family traditions and rituals are continued in an attempt to keep loved ones close. We do things because it's the way it was always done in the family. We usually don't know how traditions got started or by whom or if any parts of family traditions and rituals were revised. We know that it's the manner family celebrates and demonstrates love. Keeping traditions and rituals alive can be an attempt to recreate the warm and fuzzy feelings of love in earlier years; by doing those things remembered that made us feel connected, when all was "right in our world". We may have told ourselves that the memories were enough and that we needed to begin "new" rituals and traditions. However, the time to begin such never seemed to be quite right. Having to finally admit to not being ready to begin anew can serve as a check point for evaluating where you are on your healing journey. This point can allow one to see how far they've come while also taking note that the journey ahead to remembering the loved one with smiles and joy has yet to be reached. For your emotional wellbeing you allow yourself to process the moments of grief that have again appeared; allow it to pass, gather emotions and continue again along the journey. You must allow yourself to be alright with where you are on the healing journey, even if you have been on that journey for a number of years. Even if you feel as if for every step forward makes you take two steps backward. You will know when you are ready to replace and or revise family rituals and traditions you've known and celebrated throughout life.

How family taught us to handle life and loss will determine how we manage during our healing journey. We have observed the manner our family handled loss throughout the years and cataloged the behaviors that followed as appropriate. We observed and learned what moving forward after loss looked like in our family. We noted how females grieved in contrast to how male members of the family handled loss.

Tears and sadness may have been observed when females were grieving but what was observed in males was somewhat different. While sadness was present, rarely if ever, were tears observed in the eyes of males during such a time. Younger members of the family could "feel" the sadness of the adults and learned that death was a time of great sadness and reflection with little conversation. Yet, talking about feelings and sharing memories about the deceased can help family members navigate through a loss together. Family members can help one another through the healing journey even though each will grieve in their own way and in their own time.

Perhaps, young children were shielded from human death and were left in the care of neighbors or relatives when parents attended a funeral service. What a missed opportunity and teachable moment for young children to learn about the life cycle. Teaching children that death is a part of life assists them in better understanding and managing their grief, as death escapes no family; and no one. Our culture and family values dictate how we manage the stages of life and recovery to prepare for whatever comes next. My Pastor reminds us often that someone is facing a trial, is in the midst of a trial or was just delivered from a trial. What discussions were held in your family regarding human death, grief and mourning? What conversations were held regarding an afterlife? Was a preference discussed pertaining to burial or cremation? What discussions were held regarding the death of the family pet?

Intellectually, we know that death is part of the life cycle. But when we must deal with death on a personal level, our hearts take over. The pain of grief and that of a broken heart is too overwhelming of an emotion for most when it's personal. We were used to celebrating life, death, and most events in between with the deceased loved one. Now, we realize that we could use assistance to move forward after this death.

The Church is a great help in assisting families to prepare for each stage of life. The Church offers supports for the family through life stages via a belief system of right and wrong that supports family growth, the teaching of children, systems to assist through hardships and, when needed, counseling of families through tough times. The Church can assist families in the management of grief and beliefs of an afterlife. If we believe that our God will never leave us we are better able to get through the healing journey believing that He is beside us through the pain of grief. If we believe that He will never put more on us than we can bear, we know that He is with us through the seemingly unbearable pain of grief to a place of healing. If we believe that His grace and mercy are sufficient to get us through each day, we know that each day He is with us as we are better able to take another step toward healing. Is one of the responsibilities of the Church to prepare us for death? …of loved ones? …of our own? We know that our loved one can live forever in our memories and in our hearts; whether or not we believe in a form of eternity. The fact that a family was blessed to have their loved one for eighty, ninety, or even one hundred years is irrelevant to a broken heart. The pain of loss is not lessened because of the number of years the loved one lived and shared with others.

"Love is stronger than death even though it can't stop death from happening, but no matter how hard death tries it can't separate people from love. It can't take away our memories either. In the end, love is stronger than death."

Anonymous

DEATH IS...

The death of a parent is a real "gut wrenching" experience. "When you lose your parents, the sadness doesn't go away. It just changes. It hits you sideways sometimes instead of head-on" (**Watson, 2018**). Whatever your relationship with your parents, you will miss them when they are gone. Often when one parent dies the other follows in death soon after. Perhaps, being married for decades leaves the survivor unable to cope as being lonely and having a broken heart had become too much to bear. While children and family members were grieving and healing from the earlier death of one parent, children now add to their grieving and learn to navigate the world without either parent.

Parents rear children to leave home to become functioning adults who can contribute to society, to be of benefit to the greater good and to rear their children to do the same. While the loss of losing a parent is devasting, most children are reared with the thought that they will likely outlive their parents. The loss, though difficult, prepares one to deal emotionally with other losses in life. Parents are what grounded us, they were our roots. They were the constant in a life that now no longer exists. They were the ones who knew when things weren't quite right with us; and we often wondered how they knew. They were the ones who held our families together and knew which buttons to push to "touch" each child, although, they seldom had to go that far to secure appropriate behavior from even an adult child. Parents knew each child intimately and knew what each needed and when; even though each was very different from the other. What do we do to keep grounded when parents are no longer around? Does keeping family rituals and traditions ease the pain or bring a different pain of its own? Does holding onto sentimental possessions and memorabilia aid in educating younger generations or in generating painful memories?

The death of grandparents is the "gut wrenching" loss for the parents of the grandchildren who suffer a tragic loss. Grandparents are usually part of our formative years and were the other adults who had great influence in our growth and development. They were usually the ones who took care of us when our parents weren't around. They supported us and would often intervene when we thought our parents were being unfair in setting punishments for misbehaviors. Grandparents were the other adults who loved us unconditionally, set few behavior limits and often provided for us in manners that seemed foreign to our parents. It was the grandparent who secured dance and band lessons simply because we wanted to try a new activity. Grandmother taught us to bake and cook our favorite foods. Grandfather taught us to fish at the lake and make repairs to our favorite toys. Both grandparents taught us the benefit of growing our own garden of fresh flowers, fruits and vegetables. It was the grandparents that took us on trips to fun places without our parents. While spending time with grandparents was fun and we enjoyed the benefits of their love, we sometimes dreaded going home to where our parents were not so willing to provide extra helpings of ice cream, read extra bedtime stories or allow us to stay up past our designated bedtime. Grandparents were the ones who provided many of the "extra" things we enjoyed and gave the best hugs ever; we loved and enjoyed every moment with them. Grandparents taught a love that stays with us for the remainder of our lives. What memories do you have regarding time spent with your grandparents? What life influences do you attribute to your grandparents?

The death of a spouse is usually seen as a particularly powerful loss. One becomes a part of the other and often the surviving spouse feels as if they have lost their other half. Learning to live without the other can often be harder than expected. Many of us left our parents' home to share a home with a spouse and are usually married longer than the years spent being reared by parents. We often "grow up" with our spouse, expand careers, rear children, generate wealth and create our own world in which we learned to manage life as a couple.

There is a private language between spouses that is their secret understanding and way of managing with each other day to day. When a partner is no longer available, it is a very different world for the survivor to navigate alone. Running the household can become a daunting task. After all, tasks were a shared responsibility with each having an integral part in making the household run smoothly. Managing family needs and household responsibilities alone was never part of the plan. Now, the thought of trying to manage all the tasks seem unfair, unreal and overwhelming. Often a difference in finances, felt by the survivor, can add to an already stressful living situation. How do you continue to live and thrive in the same home shared for years without your spouse? How do you create a new existence without your greatest supporter by your side? How can the "team" continue to be successful when half of it no longer exists?

"I have lived with you and loved you, and now you are gone. Gone where I cannot follow, until I have finished all my days."

Victoria Hanley, The Seer and the Sword

17

The death of a sibling is another difficult loss. Growing up, depending on each other, having each other's back and plotting against parents became a way of survival throughout childhood. Thinking the sibling would always be around to support and love is tough when that reality does not play out. After all, Mom and Dad reared children to look out for each other, to be supportive, to keep family dynamics within, to limit information to others about family matters, sibling misbehaviors and punishments throughout maturation. Now, that sibling is no longer around to share conversations around specific memories and emotions. The death of an identical twin sibling is also like losing the other half of oneself. A friend shared that her heart was broken upon the death of her twin sister and that life would never be the same as a part of herself was now also gone. A connection with our formative past has been broken and that disconnect is felt deeply after the death of a sibling. That person could also be a son or daughter, sister or brother, grandchild, cousin, friend, classmate, or perhaps a colleague. Each one grieves for that individual differently, in their own time and in their own way. A mother grieves differently from the father for the child they created; the sister grieves differently from the brother; grandparents grieve differently from other family members; and friends grieve yet differently, depending on the closeness of that friendship. This community of grievers may be able to assist each other along their healing journeys by sharing wonderful memories and joyful stories about the deceased whenever the need to talk arises. How does one manage without the closeness of a lost sibling? How did family dynamics change after the death of a sibling?

"No matter your age or background, the process of grief is the last step in truly growing up. Life before loss was one of a kind of childlike innocence compared to the life you have now".

Westside Funeral Home Daily Support Email, February 6, 2019

The loss of dear friends brings yet a different kind of sadness and loneliness and can occur more than once in a lifetime. Dear friends are the "family" we select to go through the ups and downs of life as that dear friend simply "gets us". Many of us are closer to dear friends than we are to members of our biological family. Dear friends may know things that we are uncomfortable sharing with family members. They often know the failures and successes that had not been shared with family members. A dear friend will gladly "take to the grave" a secret she vowed to keep as you have vowed to do the same for her. Dear friends keep our secrets and often know us better than we know ourselves. We laugh, cry, argue and continue with those relationships as long as life allows. When death ends friendship we feel as if there was so much more to share about everything. We miss the interactions, excursions, talking for hours and the unsolicited opinions and advice that only a dear friend can give; advice that you may actually have given thought to considering... A void is created that is so difficult to fill that you don't try. Other friends cannot take the place of that particular loss as the bond felt appears to be irreplaceable and a new kind of sadness presents itself. While friendships change throughout life, few are held over from an early age and last throughout life. Whom will you text or speak with daily about the little things in life? Who will plan the next luncheon, girl's night out or the next girl's trip? Who will you call to go to an event when there's only one extra ticket remaining? How will you ever go shopping again without her? How have dynamics in the friendship group changed because of the loss of that friend?

The death of a loved one is a universal life changing experience. The death of a child must be the ultimate of overwhelming losses. In the scheme of life, children are likely to bury their parents; parents are not supposed to bury their children. However, when it is required that parents bury a child, the parent often feels powerless. Burying a child robs parents of the chance to mold a life, to experience and influence the hopes and dreams of that child, and to rear the child with siblings. Parents, many times, find themselves marking milestones the child could have met within their lifetime. The parents mourn the death and future of a child they did not get to know. Losing a child leaves parents with an unexplainable sadness that overtakes everything for the remainder of their lives. No matter the age of the child, parents feel a sense of responsibility for the loss. The loss of a child, whether through miscarriage or still birth, as an infant or toddler; as a teenager or adult; leaves parents to carry the burden of loss as it was their responsibility to keep their child safe. Parents often grieve the loss of a child while they care for other children who may require assistance in understanding death and grief. Much support may be needed for parents to manage their grief and that of other children in the family at the same time. Each family member will grieve in their own way, in their own time and, hopefully, will lean on each other through healing. Opportunities to talk, write or draw about feelings regarding the loss can help each family member express emotions that can lead to healing. Is there anything the parents could have done to keep their child safe? How can parents assist the rest of the family through grief and healing when they are also overwhelmed with grief?

"Death abducts the dying, but grief steals from those left behind."

Katherine Owen, Seeing Julia

"Death leaves a heartache no one can heal, love leaves a memory no one can steal".

- Anonymous

STAGES OF GRIEF

Theorists agree that there are varying stages of grief; that those grieving do not necessarily go through the stages in any particular order, and that some stages may be skipped while some may be revisited again and again (**WebMD, 2020**).

- **Denial**

  (Shock of loss, numbness of emotions)

- **Anger**

  (Frustrated, feelings of helplessness, angry at being left alone)

- **Bargaining**

  (Why did this happen? If I had only… an effort to gain some control)

- Depression

  (Sadness and regret, feelings of emptiness)

- Acceptance

  (Still sadness, seek solutions to life without your loved one)

As each person grieves in their own way and in their own time, it is understandable that one may end up spending more time in one stage of grief than another. A discussion with a counselor or a review of journal entries may give insight to what is keeping one at a particular stage of grief; especially, if one seems stuck and unable to move forward putting psychological wellness at stake. Talking with others who have experienced grief, when the need to share appears crucial, is important along the healing journey.

Young children also move through the stages of grief in their own way and in their own time after loss. Depending on the age of the child, he/she may not fully comprehend death and loss. It is up to the adults to use appropriate language, drawings and other appropriate tools to assist the child in understanding the loss that has occurred. A young child who may be able to conceptualize the loss of a goldfish may not be able to transfer that concept to the loss of a person they love. The loss of a parent, sibling or other significant adult in the child's life may require extreme patience on the part of care giving adults for the child to understand why the deceased is not returning to them as promised, yet still loves them. The services of a counselor or child psychologist may be needed to assist in dealing with the loss. While many adults have a difficult time with loss, know that children are also likely to have a difficult time and may not be capable of expressing their feelings in words. The child may only understand loss as being left behind and may revert to certain behaviors as a way of expressing feelings that they are unable to put into words. Young children may act out and or revert to age regression. Depending on the age of the child, not talking and forgetting about toileting can be a way of letting the adult in charge know that help is needed. Time and age appropriate assistance can aid children in their healing journey. One does not get over death but must assimilate and live with the loss. Have you gotten over the death of loved ones lost years ago? Recently? Each person, when living, held a special place in your heart. Now, the beloved deceased holds a cherished place in your heart and memory. Each memory and tug at your heart is filed away until someone or something causes you to remember…

How, then, does one deal with or manage grief? Does one make themselves so busy during the day that they pass out from exhaustion at day's end only to awaken in a few hours tired and irritable? Does one make themselves focus on work or a hobby so that the mind is usually occupied? The mind will not let us forget that it has a mind of its own and doesn't need us to make suggestions for it to follow. The mind grieves when it needs to do so and the body will allow it or the mind may completely shut the body down. It is important to eat properly, to get adequate rest and to be as "kind" as possible to self as the mind and body recovers from loss. It doesn't matter that we think we're busy or preoccupied; if the mind wishes, it will revisit that thing that brings the loved one to life when it so desires. The mind will remind us that we are not yet ready to return to "normal" and that additional healing time is required. At one moment we can be very focused and the next moment we may be focusing on the way a loved one reacted to a situation, favorite song or verse. Any number of circumstances can trigger memories; seeing someone in an article of clothing that resembles one owned by your loved one, a restaurant passed while driving where a favorite meal by the loved one was enjoyed, a song that you both loved dancing to, a photograph of a place visited while on vacation… There are any number of items that can and will trigger memories of your loved one and bring you to tears. Yet, other times, you won't have a clue what brought on the tears! You may have thought you were better than the day before when suddenly you realize the few steps forward toward healing seemed to have turned into numerous steps backward. You realize that your emotions are still raw and that you need additional time to be able to simply function day to day… and its OK! You will eventually notice that tears and sadness return fewer times than before. However, when the tears and sadness appear it is best to let them take over as the only way to get through the grieving process is to grieve. Whatever that looks like for you… So, let the tears flow. One day there will be fewer of them. Maybe the next day the thing that made you cry won't make you cry anymore. Maybe the thing that made you feel sad will now bring a smile to your face. Take one day at a time and notice the little steps made toward healing. Eventually, you'll notice that thing that once caused you to cry now brings joy and a smile to your face. One day you'll notice that most thoughts of your missed loved one cause you to smile. Thoughts of wonderful memories and stories will seem to flood your mind more often and you will realize that joy has replaced sadness when you think about times shared but still missed with your lost love. Eventually, you will thank God for the time you had with your loved one and your journey toward continued healing as you focus on learning to live life without him/her. Learn to be patient with yourself as you heal and struggle to regain some sense of normalcy. However, normalcy may not be what you're after since your normal had your loved one sharing life with you or at best was a text or phone call away… aim for your new normal. You will eventually find out what that looks like.

"The Lord is close to the brokenhearted and saves those who are crushed in spirit."

Psalm 34:18 NIV

"Grief is like living two lives. One is where you pretend everything is alright, and the other is where your heart silently screams in pain."

-Author Unknown

COUNSELING AND SUPPORT GROUPS

Many who grieve do not require professional assistance to manage day to day. However, it may be necessary for some to seek the services of a Grief Counselor and or Grief Support Group. A Grief Counselor has been trained in counseling the bereaved. According to Wikipedia (2020), grief counseling is a form of psychotherapy that aims to help people cope with the physical, emotional, social, spiritual, and cognitive responses to loss. A support group provides an opportunity for people to share personal experiences and feelings, coping strategies, and or firsthand information about diseases or treatments. When one finds it difficult to function in daily life and the use of alcohol and or drugs become a main focus, it may be time to seek professional help.

Support groups are available for those who prefer to talk with others who have similar experiences. Members provide each other with various types of assistance for a particular shared, usually burdensome characteristic. When members of the group share their experiences, it is often of comfort for some to hear how others are managing. Members hope that they can replicate similar behaviors in expectation of seeing some benefit for themselves. Support groups can incorporate a professional and or Christian approach to help one cope. Your minister and or physician will be able to assist you with a number of resources to research in hopes of finding the "right" group. You want the group to be a good fit for you, incorporating your beliefs and personality, as your willingness to share in a safe place will be beneficial towards your healing. Do not hesitate to locate another group if you find the group or therapist not the best fit for you.

"Grief, I've learned, is really just love. It's all the love you want to give but cannot. All of that unspent love gathers up in the corners of your eyes, the lump in your throat and in that hollow part of your chest. Grief is just love with no place to go."

-Author Unknown

JOURNALING

A journal is a written record of what you have done each day, sometimes including your private thoughts and feelings (Cambridge English Dictionary, 2020). Journaling may be a preferred method for those who prefer to write rather than speak their emotions by giving them a voice and an opportunity to be heard, even if it may be only to themselves.

Journaling allows the writer to see in black and white incremental changes occurring and have a good idea of the period when they actually experienced a breakthrough in their healing journey. The writing can be revisited at any time and as often as the writer wishes; which can be therapeutic. The writer may desire to share journal entries with a therapist or in a group counseling session. This private tool can inform the writer of specific triggers that required a revisit to deep grief as well as instances where wonderful memories emerged that encouraged happier feelings; providing of course, the writer recorded such moments. The journal can be as formal or informal as the writer wishes; from a leather bound notebook to a number of pages stapled together. The journal can be written in ink, crayon, pencil or a file created on the computer. Journaling can begin with the way one feels each day or from a prompt created by the writer or therapist. Either way, writing can be a release that can take minutes or hours to express strong feelings, emotions and or concerns along the healing journey.

"Over time, perhaps, over a number of years... I'll be able to let go of the loss. I doubt that my heart will ever let me let go of the love."

-DPHWatts

CULTURAL ASPECTS OF GRIEVING

Some cultures bury their dead in a matter of hours. Others in a matter of days. What's the customary time for grieving and or mourning in your culture? What's the difference between a funeral, a homegoing service or a New Orleans type of procession? Some cultures create an Altar in the home to honor the deceased; including items the loved one adored. Grief is a universal experience that touches all. Whatever the culture, we all display an emotion when loss is present; usually one of extreme sadness including tears. A public display of emotions may be frowned upon in some cultures and for males in other cultures. Most people demonstrate extreme sadness of loss as they find it difficult to eat, sleep and or socialize. One may indicate that they're in mourning by wearing black clothing for months, in hopes that others will let them exist in their grief. It often takes weeks after the funeral service for grieving to subside to where one can begin to focus on any sense of normalcy and begin to handle day to day events. The feeling of loss is strong no matter what one believes happens to the soul of their loved one in an afterlife. The feelings of grief must be attended to for the continued emotional and psychological health of the ones grieving. Does the lowering of the casket or the cremated remains of a body cause one to emote differently? Do cultural aspects of grieving assist in prolonging the grieving process?

"Bear ye one another's burdens and so fulfil the law of Christ."

Galatians 6:2 KJV

TRIBUTE TO YOUR LOVED ONE

One must take as long as needed to grieve, intellectually and emotionally, so that functioning day to day again becomes possible. Anniversary and holiday grief will become more manageable after the first year without your loved one. Prepare yourself for dates that are likely to trigger feelings of sadness so you are better able to manage emotionally through the years. If possible, take note of when certain dates no longer bring on tears and sadness, when your mood appears elevated and you notice feelings of joy around memories of your loved one. Realistically, a family can revisit grief several times throughout each year. Grieving can go on indefinitely, but no amount of grieving will bring back your loved one. A tribute to a loved one can encourage you to focus on an event to highlight your loved one's talents, hobby or love of giving rather than on their death. For example, tributes to beloved musicians usually focus on the legacy of their music and those influenced by it rather than on their death. Tributes for your loved one could include creating a scholarship fund in the loved one's name, purchasing a pew in memorandum in Church or a bench in a favorite park, construction of a wing in a hospital, etc. Such tributes serve to honor the deceased and educate the public of your loved one's talents or generosity for generations.

However, you publicly decide to remember and honor your deceased loved one is a very personal decision. Nothing can fill the void left by loss or lessen your love as you continue to hold a special place just for them in your heart. Time has, thank God, lessened the pain.

AUTHOR'S LAMENT

I have had the privilege of love; to love and to be loved by my late husband, parents, relatives and friends.

I am sharing a portion of my lament regarding my late husband. We were married fifteen short years as we found each other later in life. While he was a few years older than I; he was young at heart. We enjoyed playing tennis, traveling, having a glass of wine on the patio, playing backgammon, and each other's company as we were both retired for much of our marriage. We walked the shores of beaches we visited while on vacation and even talked of moving to the east coast where we'd be better able to enjoy outdoor activities year round. He was not a complainer and would rarely inform anyone, even me, that he was not feeling his best. As he aged, he was unable to play tennis as in earlier years or even walk as far along the shores of the beaches we visited. Doctors suggested a hip replacement to ease mobility and pain concerns. After some discussion, the surgery was scheduled. He was alert and seemed well after surgery. We were happy to give thought to making plans soon to enjoy the outdoors again. However, the day after surgery a complication arose. Therapists and specialists were called to consult. The complications had nothing to do with the surgery, per se, but with a likely injury from numerous years past; which surgery protocols likely irritated. My husband was having difficulty swallowing which led to aspiration which led to difficulty breathing. That led to a transfer to another hospital better suited to care for his needs. After two months in the hospital, several surgeries, placement on a ventilator, insertion of a feeding tube, and a diagnosis of sepsis, life became very different for us. Our ministers, family and friends were with us through most of his hospitalization and were with me as we stood by his bedside during his final life moments. I was holding his hand when I felt life drain from him; a moment I will never forget. I am grateful that we were with him and that I had the comfort of others at that moment. His death is forever a part of my being. I don't know how I could have made it through

41

that day without my ministers, family and friends by my side. They continue to check to find out how I'm managing through my healing journey. Some days are easier than others; I know that I am headed towards healing as I can look back to acknowledge the pain from which I've come. Yet, I am very much aware that there is still much healing ahead. There are moments when I still need to talk things through with others who have faced a similar journey. I'm so grateful that they are available to me with continued words of encouragement. I thank God for placing people in my life that have been a great source of comfort along the way.

"Grief never ends. But it changes. It's a passage not a place to stay. Grief is not a sign of weakness, nor a lack of faith. It is the price of love."

Author Unknown

CONTINUED HEALING

I pray continued healing for you as you take the necessary time to grieve, talk with a friend, consult a counselor, join a support group, or journal your way to the new you. May your new normal allow you to love, smile, build relationships and live life with happiness and joy in your spirit.

Not a day goes by that I don't think of those that are no longer available for me to reach out and touch because of loss. I still love them. I still miss them. I still hold a special place for each one of them in my heart. I am forever changed because of the losses but honored to have known and learned from each one. Loving parents, a loving spouse, loving relatives and loving friendships… each taught a different lesson about love, each left an indelible imprint on my heart. Each claimed a part of me and my experiences with each created the person that remains. I thank God daily for His grace, His mercy and His love.

FOOTPRINTS IN THE SAND

One night I dreamed a dream.

As I was walking along the beach with my Lord.

Across the dark sky flashed scenes from my life.

For each scene, I noticed two sets of footprints in the sand,

One belonging to me and one to my Lord.

After the last scene of my life flashed before me,

I looked back at the footprints in the sand.

I noticed that at many times along the path of my life,

especially at the very lowest and saddest times,

there was only one set of footprints.

This really troubled me, so I asked the Lord about it.

"Lord, you said once I decided to follow you,

You'd walk with me all the way.

But I have noticed that during the saddest times of my life,

there was only one set of footprints.

I don't understand why, when I needed You the most, you would leave me."

He whispered, "My precious child, I love you and I will never leave you

Never, ever, during your trials and testings.

When you saw only one set of footprints,

It was then that I carried you."

Author Unknown

REFERENCES

Ecclesiastes 3:1-8. ASV. In BibleGateway.com

Footprints in the sand, a beautiful poem. Onlythebible.com. April 24, 2020.

Galatians 6:2. KJV. In BibleRef.com

Grief counseling definition. In Wikipedia search. en.m.wikipedia.org. March 2020.

Hanley, V. The sear and the sword. Westside Funeral Grief Support Email, October 19, 2018

Journal definition. In dictionary.cambridge.org. April 22, 2020.

Mourning definition. In Goggle search. February 2020.

"No matter your age or background…" Westside Funeral Home Daily Support Email, February 6, 2019.

Owen, K. Seeing Julia. Westside Funeral Home Daily Grief Support Email. March 31, 2019.

Psalms 34:18. NIV. In BibleGateway.com

Psychotherapy definition. In Wikipedia search. May 2020

Watson, J. In too deep. Westside Funeral Home Daily Grief Support Email. October 20, 2018.

What are the stages of grief? In Webmd.com. March 2020.

100 inspiring quotes by Alfred Lord Tennyson that will brighten up your day. Google.com. April 24, 2020.

TERMS

Bereaved: to be deprived of a loved one through a profound absence, especially due to the loved one's death

Grieve: to feel or express great sorrow, usually emotionally, especially when someone dies

Mourning: the expression of deep sorrow, usually publicly, for someone who has died

Psychotherapy: the talking therapy, use of psychological methods, particularly when based on regular personal interaction with adults, to help a person change behavior and overcome problems in desired ways

Notes

Notes

Notes

_____

_____

_____

_____

_____

_____

_____

_____

_____

_____

_____

_____

_____

_____

Notes

ABOUT THE AUTHOR

Deborah Hammond-Watts holds a doctorate in educational administration. She has served as an elementary school teacher, school administrator, elementary school principal, adjunct professor, author contributor to college texts, and has volunteered in non-profit agencies. Deborah has a passion for traveling, exercising, reading, helping others, and serving her Church community.